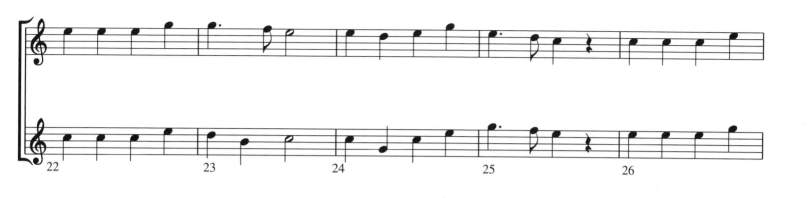

Away In A Manger

Alto Saxophones

With Movement

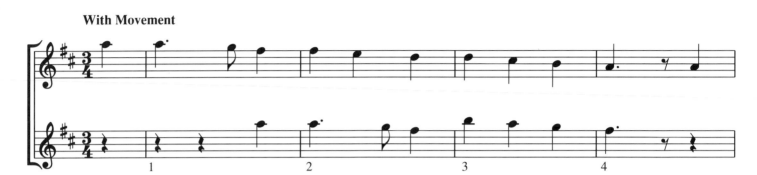

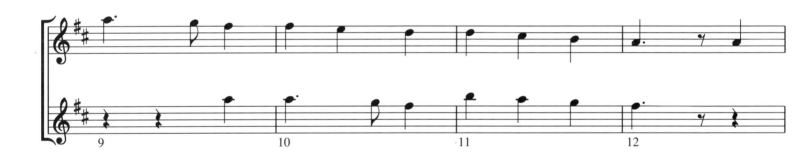

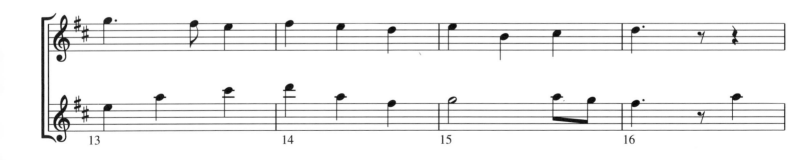

CHRISTMAS CAROLS FOR TWO

EASY DUETS

HAL•LEONARD®
CORPORATION

7777 W. BLUEMOUND RD. P.O. BOX 13819 MILWAUKEE, WI 53213

Angels We Have Heard On High

Alto Saxophones

Brightly

5

Deck The Hall

Alto Saxophones

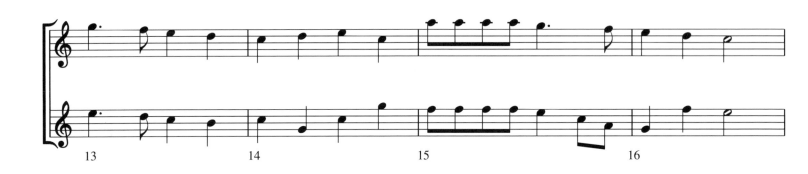

The First Noel

Alto Saxophones

God Rest Ye Merry, Gentlemen

Alto Saxophones

With Movement

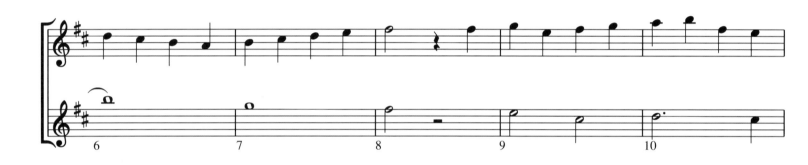

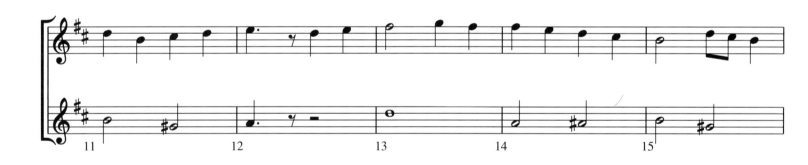

Hark! The Herald Angels Sing

Alto Saxophones

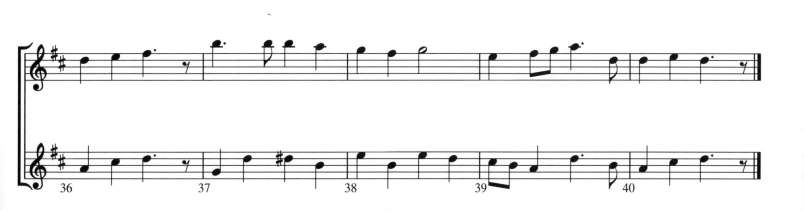

It Came Upon The Midnight Clear

Alto Saxophones

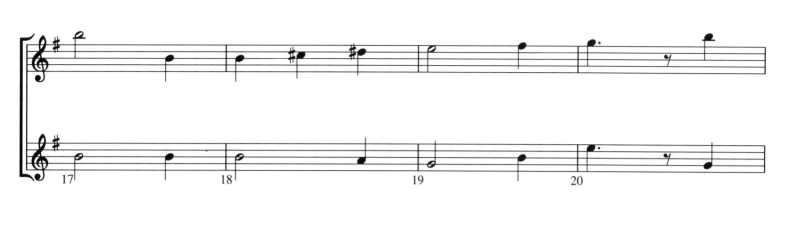

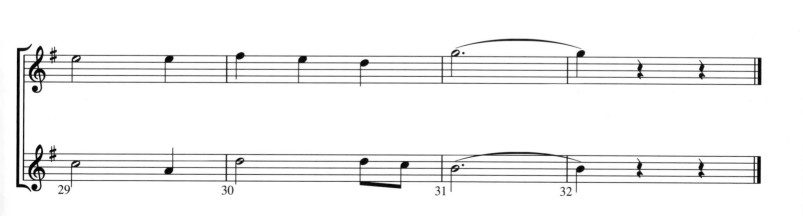

Jolly Old St. Nicholas

Alto Saxophones

Lively

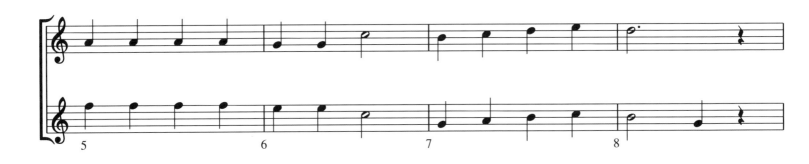

Joy To The World

Alto Saxophones

Lively

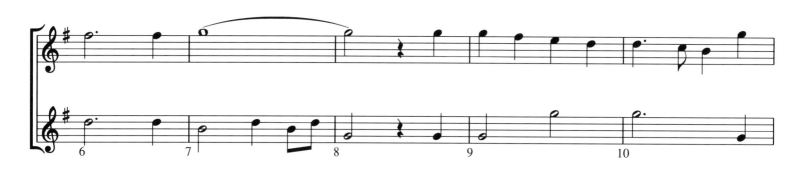

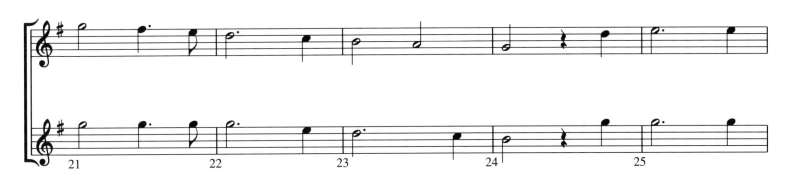

O Holy Night

Alto Saxophones

O Little Town Of Bethlehem

Alto Saxophones

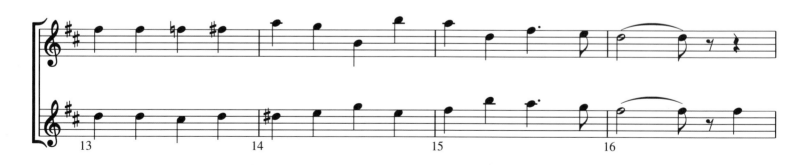

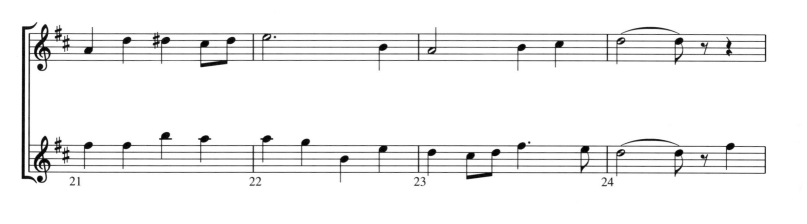

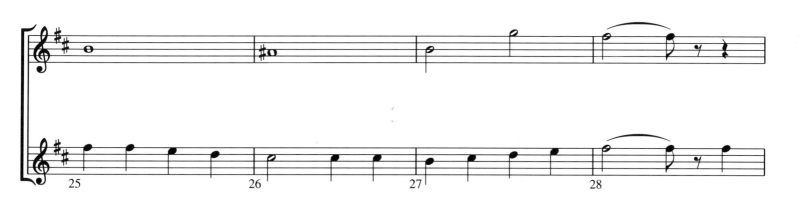

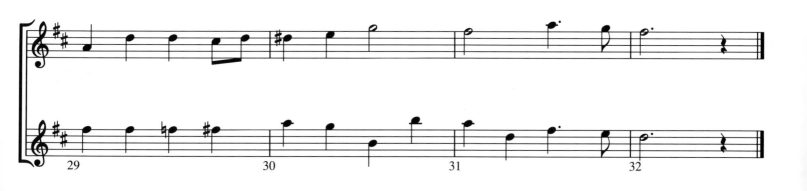

Silent Night

Alto Saxophones

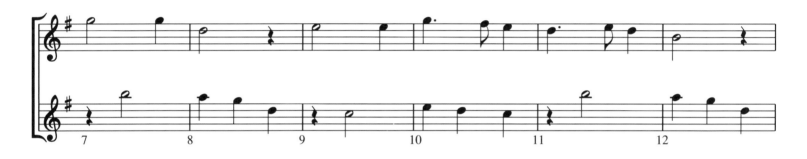

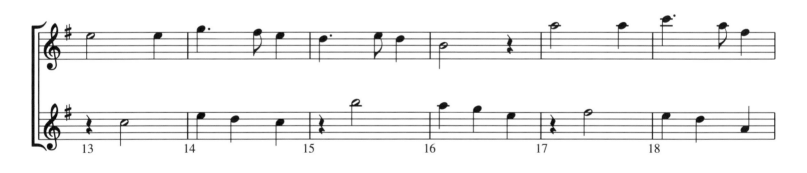

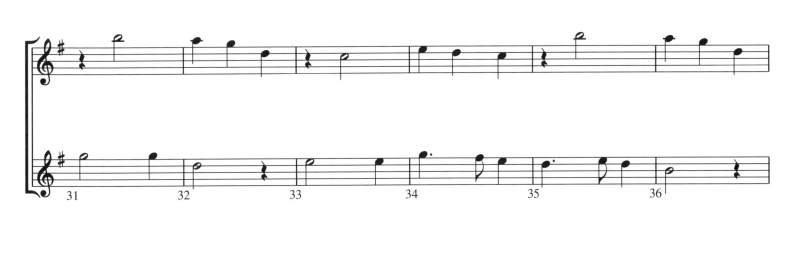

We Three Kings Of Orient Are

Alto Saxophones

Brightly

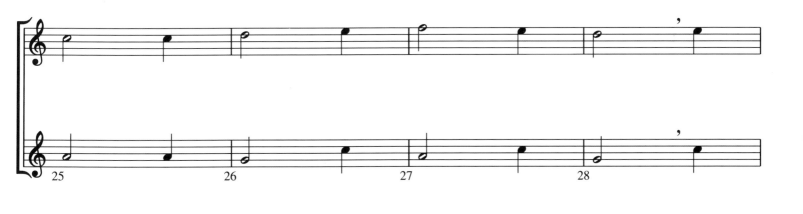

We Wish You A Merry Christmas

Alto Saxophones

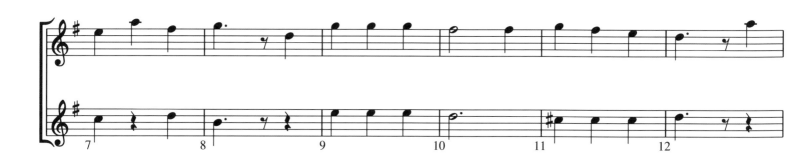

What Child Is This?

Alto Saxophones

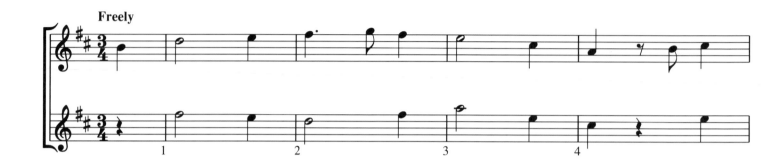

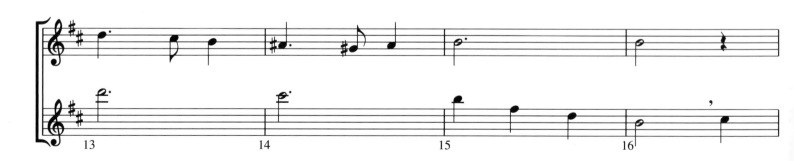